*God's Pathway
to Healing*

THE IMMUNE
SYSTEM

BOOKS BY
REGINALD B. CHERRY, M.D.

GOD'S PATHWAY TO HEALING:

Bone Health

Diabetes

Digestion

Heart

Herbs That Heal

The Immune System

Joints and Arthritis

Memory and Mental Acuity

Menopause

Prostate

Vision

Vitamins and Supplements

Dr. Cherry's Little Instruction Book

*God's Pathway
to Healing*

THE IMMUNE
SYSTEM

by

Reginald B. Cherry, M.D.

BETHANYHOUSE
Minneapolis, Minnesota

God's Pathway to Healing: The Immune System
Copyright © 2003
Reginald B. Cherry, M.D.

Manuscript prepared by Rick Killian, Killian Creative,
Boulder, Colorado. *www.killiancreative.com*

Cover design by Danielle White

Note: The directions given in this book are in no way to be
considered a substitute for consultation with your own
physician.

Scripture credits appear at the end of the book as a
continuation of the copyright page.

Italics in Scripture quotes denote author emphasis.

Published by Bethany House Publishers
11400 Hampshire Avenue South
Bloomington, Minnesota 55438

Bethany House Publishers is a Division of
Baker Book House Company, Grand Rapids, Michigan.

Printed in the United States of America

ISBN 0-7642-2835-8

CONTENTS

Introduction........................... 9

1. God's Miraculous Gift to Us:
    The Immune System 11

2. How the Immune System Functions... 29
    Problems Develop When the
        Immune System Becomes
        Imbalanced 41
    Putting Glasses on the Immune
        System 44

3. Lifestyle for a Healthy Immune
    System........................... 47
    Proper Nutrition................. 51
        The Mediterranean Diet....... 53
        Other Foods Beneficial to
            Immune System Balance ... 62

Soy Products 62

Pomegranates 63

Maitake, Reishi, and
Shiitake Mushrooms 63

Avoid Foods that Stimulate the
Immune System If You Are
Facing Autoimmune
Disease 67

Alfalfa Sprouts 67

Shellfish and Zinc 68

Corn, Safflower, and
Sunflower Oils 68

Exercise 69

Determine Your Safe Heart-
Rate Range 72

Weight Management 73

Coping With Stress and Grief 74

God's Plan for Healthy Living 76

4. Vitamins and Supplements for
Immune System Support 79

Basic Nutritional Support 84

Other Vitamins and Supplements
    for Immune System Health 85
  Vitamins...................... 85
      Vitamin E 86
      Vitamin C 87
      Vitamin A (from beta
        carotene) 87
  Minerals
    Copper...................... 87
    Selenium 88
    Zinc 89
  Herbs
    Astragalus 89
    Garlic...................... 90
Other Extracts and Compounds
    Blueberries 91
    Elderberries 91
    Pomegranate Seed 91
    Mushrooms.................. 92
    Beta 1, 3 Glucan 93
    Lactobacillus Sporogenes 94
    Arabinigalactan 95

Glucono-Delta-Lactone....... 95

L-Glutamine 96

Inulin...................... 96

Olive Leaf Extract............ 96

Siberian Ginseng Root Extract .. 97

Echinacea and Goldenseal Are
Best Used Short-Term..... 97

We All Need a Balanced and
Healthy Immune System 98

5. Your Daily Walk on the Pathway
to a Healthy and Vibrant Immune
System....................... 99

God Has a Unique Pathway to Health
for You 109

Endnotes 113

Reginald B. Cherry, M.D.—
A Medical Doctor's Testimony 117

About the Author..................... 121

Resources Available From
Reginald B. Cherry Ministries, Inc.... 123

Become a Pathway to Healing Partner.... 135

INTRODUCTION

When God first created man and woman in the Garden of Eden, He gave humankind an incredible gift to fight disease—the immune system. Science is only now, in fact, beginning to understand the healing power locked inside this system when it is allowed to function unhindered. Research is finding that our immune system not only fights foreign bacteria, viruses, colds, the flu, and allergies, but also does a great deal to eliminate cancer, tumors, and other chronic illnesses. Immune system function is truly an everyday healing miracle.

However, if this is true, why do people still get sick? It is because the things we take into our bodies—food, smoke, pollutants, pollens, and mold, etc.—can throw our immune system into imbalances that impair its function. An overactive immune system can cause allergies, chronic fatigue, asthma, and rheumatoid arthritis, among other things, while an underactive immune system can allow colds and the flu, viral disorders, and even hepatitis and cancer. The key to a strong and effective immune system is balance.

How do we maintain that balance? Well, that is what this pocket book is all about. In the following pages we will discuss the wonder of God's design of the immune system, how it works, what impairs it, and how to keep it working properly.

We are indeed fearfully and wonderfully made! Because of that, the first step for all of us in God's plan for healthy living is a strong, balanced immune system.

—Reginald B. Cherry, M.D.

Chapter 1

GOD'S MIRACULOUS GIFT TO US: THE IMMUNE SYSTEM

Chapter 1

GOD'S MIRACULOUS GIFT TO US: THE IMMUNE SYSTEM

So God created man in His own image; in the image of God He created him; male and female He created them. . . . And God said, "See, I have given you every herb that yields seed which is on the face of all the earth, and every tree whose fruit yields seed; to you it shall be for food." . . . Then God saw everything that He had made, and indeed it was very good. (Genesis 1:27, 29, 31 NKJV)

I will praise thee; for I am fearfully and

wonderfully made: marvelous are thy
works; and that my soul knoweth right
well. (Psalm 139:14)

We are truly fearfully and wonderfully
made. Many think that science contradicts the
Bible, but the truth is that science is just catch-
ing up with the Bible. Science is only scratch-
ing the surface of how truly miraculous God's
design is. This is especially true in the case of
medical science and the dietary laws of the Old
Testament. Research has come a long way to
confirm that the Bible's dietary laws and the
foods God provided for His children in Israel
are great keys to keeping our bodies healthy!
Why is this diet so healthy? One of the reasons
is that it strengthens and balances our immune
system.

In Exodus 23:25–26, God said that He
would put His blessing on our food and water
and take sickness from the midst of us. In other
words, He tied health to His blessing on our

food. Medical science is now confirming that our best defense against disease and chronic illness is simply to eat the right things and avoid eating the wrong things. When looking for a guideline for that, the Mediterranean diet (which we will discuss in more detail in chapter 3) has provided the best outline.

When we eat the right foods and take the right supplements, the immune system's function is no less than an everyday miracle. In fact, nothing has baffled medical science more in recent decades—other than instantaneous, miraculous healings—than the incredible function of the immune system.

One example of this was recorded in medical journals from the mid–1960s. It was the case of a man named Harold White. He was a fifty-five-year-old body shop mechanic who lived in Pennsylvania. He was having some trouble breathing, so he went in for a checkup. As a result, they referred him to another doctor, who recommended some X-rays be taken. The

X-rays showed an enlarged lymph node above his right collarbone. They looked at other X-rays and found a shadowy spot in his right lung. It was a tumor. So they decided he needed a biopsy. A small portion of the swollen lymph node was removed and the tissue went up to the pathology department. (Pathologists are the M.D.'s who look under microscopes and make the diagnosis of whether a growth is benign or malignant—in other words, harmless or cancerous.) The report whistled back down to the operating room like a bombshell. They took one look at the slide and said, "small-cell carcinoma"—a very aggressive and deadly form of lung cancer. In fact, upon further research they found it was "oat-cell carcinoma," for which there is no known treatment. In cases like this, the patient survives a few months at the most.

So they told Mr. White he had a tumor and that there was nothing they could do for him. The tumor was completely inoperable and incurable, and the symptoms were minimal, so there was nothing to be gained by any treatments. Mr. White was sent from the hospital in 1966 with the prognosis of only a few months to live.

However, in 1971 Mr. White returned to the hospital. If the same doctors saw him, they must have thought they were seeing a ghost! This time Mr. White complained of soreness in his shoulder. The radiology department went into high gear. They pulled out his old X-rays and examined them again—there was definitely a mass in his lungs. No question about it. However, after examining the new X-rays taken in 1971, the flabbergasted radiologist wrote on the new films, "Mass is not present; absolutely not present."

The odd thing is that when something as miraculous as this happens, rather than believing their own eyes and rejoicing with patients at their healing, doctors often look to place blame, accusing one another of making a mistake. In this case, the radiologist in 1971 suggested that the pathologist in 1966 had misdiagnosed the patient—in other words, he had been completely wrong! If that doctor's diagnosis had been correct, this man could not have been alive in 1971!

Of course, the pathologist who first took the case was upset about this accusation. His response was, "How dare you accuse us of missing the diagnosis. We do have the slides from 1966."

So they pulled the slides from Mr. White's 1966 biopsy and reviewed them. Then they sent them to two other outside hospital departments to review the slides. The response was unanimous: The slides showed small-cell carcinoma, and the patient should have been dead within six months. However, here he was five years later very much alive, with only a minor ache in his shoulder and no sign of cancer. The ache in his shoulder, by the way, turned out to be arthritis, which the doctors were able to treat easily.

Still not able to believe the results, the doctors sent copies of the biopsy slides and X-rays to cancer experts across the country and published the images in medical literature. No one yet has disputed their conclusions. The man should have been dead before 1967. Yet there he was in 1971.

There is no evidence in any of the reports that would indicate the man was a believer or that he had been ministered to by believers, though I don't doubt that someone hearing of his first diagnosis prayed for him. However, from the evidence in the journals it appears that he had a miraculous recovery by the miracle planted inside him at his birth—his immune system.

And this was no fluke occurrence. There are other amazing examples of this recorded in medical journals. A similar case is that of twelve-year-old William Blow. Originally his symptoms sounded like a bout of tonsillitis. He had a sore throat, and his tonsils were swollen.

He also had a lymph node that had enlarged in his neck. He went to the hospital, and the emergency room doctor snipped off a portion of the tonsil for a biopsy. The biopsy showed that he had a rapidly growing tumor known as a high-grade lymphoma. He was referred to the hospital.

He reported there in July 1984. The lymph node was now the size of an apricot and was growing rapidly. The doctor and pathologist took another biopsy and confirmed the original diagnosis. High-grade lymphoma is actually an unusually aggressive cancer of the immune system. Normally these types of tumors double in size every few days; however, here is where the amazing part of the story comes in: The tumor did not grow, and after two days in the hospital, it actually began to get smaller.

Now, this put the doctors in a very peculiar situation. Normally this type of tumor calls for very aggressive treatment—usually chemotherapy—and that was what William had been admitted to the hospital for, yet if it was getting smaller rather than bigger, should it even be treated? Doctors tend to want to do something—and in cases of cancer, they typically blast it with chemotherapy as quickly as possible. It is very awkward to just sit and wait. The doctors argued back and forth, and finally decided to do nothing. "As long as it got smaller," they reasoned, "we felt we could wait. And the more we waited, the smaller it got."

Here they had a young boy with a devastating form of lymphoma, an immune-system cancer—normally fatal if it is not treated quickly enough, and they decided to wait to treat it—to see what would happen. And that decision turned out to be the correct one; the tumor got smaller and smaller until it finally disappeared all on its own!

Seven years after being admitted to the hospital, when William Blow was almost twenty, he was checked out and given a clean bill of health. There was no sign that he had ever had lymphoma. They wrote his story up in *Cancer*, a widely distributed medical journal. Despite the evidence, one of the doctors to this day thinks the original diagnosis was wrong, even though two different biopsies from different pathologists confirmed it was correct.

Now, what am I telling you here? I want you to understand this: Whatever you have in your body; whatever doctors have told you, I want you to know of these two cases of the worst illnesses seen in medicine that totally disappeared, with doctors having no idea how, except that something in each person's body dissolved the tumor and healed the patient. It might be that praying believers were involved in the background—I don't doubt that there were; who wouldn't pray for someone who received such a diagnosis?—but we have no firm evidence in these articles. We have no knowledge that the patients were Christians. The point is that these are documented cases in medical literature of healings that are so unbelievable that doctors accused one another of having made the wrong diagnoses. Yet all the evidence points to the diagnoses being correct; and these people who were possibly within months of death, lived long full lives afterward. They were absolutely healed of these cancers, and no trace of them remained in their bodies.

Another such report tells of a patient who staggered into a VA hospital in January 1967 with a 104-degree temperature. When they tested him, they found that his bloodcell count was extremely low. When they did a biopsy of his bone marrow, they found that he had acute myelocytic leukemia, one of the worst forms. With this type of leukemia, if the patient doesn't respond well to treatment, he will die within three to twelve months.

So the doctors decided to begin chemotherapy. They put the patient on two different drugs, with a dosage of 50 milligrams, QID (four times a day). A new intern who took over the case ten days later, however, read the treatment "QD" (once a day). So instead of getting the four treatments of chemotherapy per day as originally prescribed, the patient received his treatment only once a day—one fourth the medication doctors thought he needed.

Nevertheless, his blood count started coming up to normal. He was less anemic, and he started getting better. Over the next two weeks, his fever broke and normal color returned to his face. Yet the most startling transformation of all was to be seen only with a microscope. All the abnormal cells that were choking his bone marrow had vanished—totally gone.

Today we know, through modern research, that the two medicines prescribed for this man are not effective for treating this form of leukemia. The treatment at that time was somewhat experimental, but they felt they had to do something. Thank God, due to the "error" in reading the prescription, the dosage was small enough that the man did not have complications because of the treatment—which is something that happens too frequently.

The journal goes on to state that after two months of getting a quarter of the prescribed ineffective chemotherapy treatment, this fellow walked out of the hospital and embarked on the second part of his life, and has never relapsed. Twenty-five years later he was alive and well and still writing Christmas cards to his doctor.

Such cases only add to the argument that it doesn't matter what you are facing—there can be a way out for you. You must have hope.

Now, these stories are from natural, scientific medical journals—these are not healing testimonies from a ministry's magazine. If such things can happen without evidence that God was involved, how much more can we have confidence when we have God's healing promises in His Word?

> *He sent his word, and healed them,* and delivered them from their destructions. (Psalm 107:20)

But he was wounded for our transgressions, he was bruised for our iniquities: the chastisement of our peace was upon him; and *with his stripes we are healed.* (Isaiah 53:5)

They went forth, and preached every where, the Lord working with them, and *confirming the word with signs following.* (Mark 16:20)

God wants to confirm His Word to us, and these cases are confirmations of God at work through the everyday miracle of our immune system, documented by medical journals.

Some people are skeptical of healing testimonies in Christian magazines. They may think things like, "Maybe the person thought they were healed and really weren't," or "They just make that stuff up to get people to send money"; but you can't argue with documented cases in medical journals. Doctors have not been able to argue with such cases, either.

There is a reason that all of these things are taking place—a spiritual reason.

God gave us all a gift at creation to keep us healthy: the immune system. Scientists are only beginning to understand the natural side of this gift. They are starting to recognize that such cases of healing are because of the immune system at work. They still are not sure exactly how it works.

I believe the immune system is at the center of miracles like these—the natural sign of God's healing gift within us. I believe God can supernaturally heal any illness or disease through a sovereign touch of His will, but I also believe that more often than not His healings come as the result of the natural elements He gave us to stay healthy—not only the immune and other systems within us, but also plants and herbs and fruits and vegetables that provide natural remedies to some of the most chronic illnesses and diseases. In many cases, God designed our immune system to fight off these ailments. We should be praying and standing on His Word and His promises for our healing, but we should also be acting on the natural wisdom we have to help our immune system fight whatever we might face.

As you may have noticed, the cases cited above are from twenty or thirty years ago. As a result of such cases, more research has been done in recent years on how the immune system functions and the best ways to keep it balanced and strong. In the following chapters we will look at how the immune system functions, what foods and natural supplements help keep it functioning properly, and how the immune system may well be part of God's pathway to healing whatever ailments or health concerns you or a loved one may be facing.

Chapter 2

HOW THE IMMUNE SYSTEM FUNCTIONS

Chapter 2

HOW THE IMMUNE SYSTEM FUNCTIONS

In studying the immune system, we see the hand of God reaching down to protect us—for in the immune system God gave us a literal everyday miracle. While it may well be the most important system in the body, it is also one of the least understood, perhaps because of its complexity and its integration with other systems in our body. Despite its complexity, however, its purpose is concise and clear: to block or eliminate foreign or strange organisms that invade our bodies and cause disease.

Daily we are exposed to numerous things that could make us sick. Medical science calls these disease-causing invaders *antigens,* which tag along into the body on *pathogens,* more traditionally known as *germs.* Antigens are basically anything that enters the body and stimulates the production of antibodies. Among these are bacteria, microbes, viruses, toxins, parasites, and fungi, and within these groups are various strains of each as they adapt and change, or are imported from different environments. This is why each year we face a new version of the flu, and there is a new round of flu shots suggested to prevent it. It is also why the common cold still has no cure—the "cold-causing" pathogens change so rapidly that we can only treat the symptoms. We get sick because somehow these viruses or bacteria penetrate our immune system's defenses and affect us on a cellular level. In contrast, we get better because our immune system adapts itself to combat these invaders and eliminates them from our bodies through fever, cellular counterattacks, inflammation, and other means of killing and then flushing trespassers from our systems.

Components of the immune system range from the epidermis (the surface of the skin) to the thymus, which lies between the breastbone and the heart and regulates the production of T cells—an integral part of the cellular defense of the immune system. These components fight sickness in primarily two ways.

The first is *innate immunity,* which is the body's first and most general line of defense, and because of this is also called *nonspecific immunity.* The parts of the immune system that function in this way are those that fight to keep foreign objects from entering our system in the first place. The skin is a good example of this. The skin acts as a protective shield to keep things out of our body and also secretes anti-bacterial substances that kill invaders when they land on us. When the skin is cut or punctured by something like a splinter, we are open to infection and disease. At this, the innate immune system rushes to kill any infectious invaders to prevent them from penetrating further into our body. If the infection persists, pus may form, which is mostly made up of dead white blood cells that have spent themselves trying to kill the infection. The area will also swell to increase the flow of blood and other body fluids to help wash away the dead cells and infection-causing pathogens. Other examples of components of this line of defense are tears, saliva, and mucus, which all trap invaders and work to "wash" or filter foreign organisms and objects from our bodies.

The other type of immunity is *adaptive* or *acquired immunity*. This is the second line of defense against disease and handles all the invaders that find entrance into the body. It is called *adaptive, acquired,* or *specific immunity* because it can look at an antigen, determine if it is harmful, and adapt itself to effectively eliminate each specific invader from our body.

Adaptive immunity has four basic properties:

(1) It only responds once it recognizes an invader is present.

(2) Its response is "tailor-made" to address the specific antigen recognized.

(3) It remembers how it deals with each invader, and responds better to the disease-causing agent the next time it faces it, even if it is some time later.

(4) It normally does not attack healthy body components, but only what it recognizes as foreign and potentially harmful.

This level of immunity is also what vaccinations depend upon. We are given a small dose of dead elements of a disease or a weaker, similar form of it, and our immune system adapts to defeat that and eliminate it from our bodies. Then, if and when the real, live disease comes along, our immune system remembers how it dealt effectively with the vaccine, and we never develop any of the harmful effects of those diseases because the invaders are thwarted before we ever develop symptoms.

The adaptive immune system functions in primarily two ways: *humoral* or *cell mediated*. Humoral immune responses are when antibodies attack antigens in the blood and other body fluids. They attack the invaders before they enter into or interact with the body's cells. Cell-mediated immune responses are when the immune system releases cells that will capture or destroy other cells that have been infected by disease-causing agents. This is the part of the immune system that recognizes "sick" or cancerous cells and eliminates them, stopping cancer before it is even noticed by us or by doctors. Some researchers have hypothesized that each of us probably develops cancerous cells at least once every few days, but that our cell-mediated immune responses systematically eliminate the cells before they cause problems.

Our immune system uses a myriad of components to adapt and defeat disease in this way in order to keep us healthy. As I said before, scientists don't understand every detail of how it all works, but researchers have been able to identify many of the key players in the process and what they do. A cursory understanding of these will help in our later discussions of ways to keep the immune system functioning properly and effectively.

While the intricacies of immune function are incredibly varied and complex, the overall pattern appears somewhat uniform. A variety of white blood cells, antibodies, compliment system proteins, and other immune system agents—each specifically designed to tag or kill a specific antigen invader—regularly flow through our blood and body fluids looking to head off disease before it can strike. Under each of these categories are a multitude of subgroups that have special configurations to fight disease. Many of these agents begin as *stem cells* that are produced in the bone marrow and go on to become B cells or T cells, depending on whether they mature in the bones or the thymus. White and red blood cells are also produced in the bone marrow. Antibodies (the y-shaped proteins that attack antigens) are produced by the white blood cells. White blood cells can also change into lymphocytes, helper T cells, killer T cells, NK (natural killer) cells, macrophages ("big eater" cells that consume pathogens), neutrophils, eosinophils, and basophils, among several others. Our systems can also trigger the production of more of each of these as needed to face invasions. Major histocompatibility complex molecules (more commonly called MHC molecules) tag antigens to be attacked by other immune agents such as the killer T cells.

As a whole, these agents have varying functions: some tag suspect cells so that others will attack them; some will kill the antigens; compliment system proteins attack and burst diseased cells so that other agents can work on them; while others, such as macrophages, envelop the pathogens or diseased cells in a process called *phagocytosis* (which means literally "cell eating") to capture the invaders and drag them to a place where they will be filtered and eliminated from the body. Immune-system hormones, collectively called *lymphokines,* are also produced by the immune system to trigger the production of other immune system agents, tell the hypothalamus to raise the body temperature, or signal other organs to help fight the disease.

Once these immune system agents have done their jobs, the invaders are "washed" from our bodies through the lymph system, the blood, the spleen, the tonsils, or other filtering organs. The lymph system does a good deal of its disease fighting in the lymph nodes, junctures of the lymph system that filter the lymph fluid. When infection or disease is present in the body, areas such as the lymph nodes or tonsils will swell as they become filled with the pathogens they are filtering and the agents attacking them. This is why doctors check the lymph nodes in your neck if you complain of cold or flu symptoms—they are checking for signs that your immune system is fighting something. This is also why drinking lots of liquids is good when facing a cold or the flu; the extra fluids help wash illness from our bodies.

So the basic pattern is that the agents of the immune system capture or kill the antigens, and then filter them out of the body, though the methods of doing this seem to vary and adapt almost as quickly as the invaders do. The effectiveness of this system is perhaps best seen, however, in the fact that most of us stay healthy most of the time, all while our immune system is constantly fighting invading pathogens. Only rarely does it meet a challenge it can't handle in less than a few days' time. This is why colds and flu generally only last a couple of days. More serious problems are faced, however, when the immune system is weakened or over-stimulated.

PROBLEMS DEVELOP WHEN THE IMMUNE SYSTEM BECOMES IMBALANCED

What short-circuits the immune system and begins to cause problems for us, is when it starts to get imbalanced: either as a result of overactivity, such as when immune system agents attack healthy tissue or invaders that are not disease-causing, or underactivity as the system begins to slow down and becomes overwhelmed so that it does not react quickly enough to invaders or cancerous cells that can become life threatening.

It is quite normal for our immune system to start to slow down as we get older unless we work actively to counteract this effect of age. By the age of fifty-five or sixty, almost every person who has been studied has shown a significant decline in their immune function, and this begins to throw the door open to an incredible list of diseases. Other factors can lead to the decline of the immune systems in younger people as well, the most blatant example of which is AIDS. This disease directly attacks immune function and usually does not kill the patient, but allows something that would not normally be deadly to develop into something fatal. Because the immune system is weakened by the HIV virus, it is less apt to fight off these lesser ailments. A less-active immune system can be responsible for anything from more frequent and severe colds and flus to other viral disorders, hepatitis, pneumonia, and the ultimate failure of the immune system: cancer. The more weakened and slow the immune system is to respond, the more common conditions can grow to dangerous proportions.

On the other end of this spectrum is an *overactive* immune system. Perhaps the best and most common example of this is allergies. For some reason, the immune system becomes hyper-vigilant and begins to identify harmless invaders as disease-causing, which is why allergies are also called *hypersensitivity*. This results in common pollens, pet dander, certain foods, and the like triggering the immune system to go into overdrive, flooding the nasal passages with mucus, inflaming glands, and causing us to sneeze, all in the hope of ejecting the invaders, which really don't need all that attention. One of the things that causes all of this fuss is the unwarranted release of histamines, which is why most allergy drugs contain antihistamines. While these do relieve the bothersome symptoms of allergies, they don't address the actual cause—the overactive immune system. Other things that are caused by a hyper-vigilant immune system are asthma and chronic fatigue syndrome.

Another class of overactive immune disorder is the autoimmune diseases: this is when the immune system attacks the cells of our own bodies. Multiple sclerosis, for example, is a disease in which the immune system attacks the nervous system, beginning with the myelin sheaths that protect the nerves and their communication centers. Rheumatoid arthritis is when the immune system starts attacking the joints. Still other disorders caused by an overactive immune system are fibromyalgia, lupus, scleroderma, and inflammatory bowel diseases such as Crohn's disease, ileitis, and so on. Somehow, because of our modern poor nutrition, overload of pollutants and other invaders, general lack of exercise, and other factors we have yet to identify, the immune system panics and begins attacking its own allies instead of its enemies.

PUTTING GLASSES ON THE IMMUNE SYSTEM

In answer to most of these problems, however, medical science is looking for more powerful drugs rather than a way to bring the immune system back into balance and let it do its job correctly. This is why taking things like Echinacea that stimulate the immune system is not the answer, although it might help in the short-term treatment of colds, the flu, and the like. We don't want a constantly stimulated immune system any more than we want a subdued and toned-down immune system. What we want is a balanced immune system, or as some have said, "We want to put glasses on the immune system."

What does that mean? Just as we put corrective lenses on a person who is near- or far-sighted, we need to put glasses on the immune system so that it properly "sees" what it should respond to and what it should not respond to. Glasses "correct" vision by bringing it back to a normal range, and that is what we need to do with the immune system. It needs to be balanced, and it needs to be able to "see" clearly.

It is amazing to me how often God gives us a simple solution to a complex group of problems. Think about this for a moment: If we could address all of these different diseases by just bringing the immune system back into balance, wouldn't that be an amazingly simple answer for medical science? But because individuals vary so much, and pathogens adapt and change so readily, it is hard to say if this would be a cure-all for all diseases, but it may very well be that balancing the immune system is part of God's pathway to healing for many of the health concerns you may be facing. Now that we understand God's everyday miracle of the immune system a little better, let's look at some of the things we can do to bring it back into balance and allow it to keep us healthier.

Chapter 3

LIFESTYLE FOR A HEALTHY IMMUNE SYSTEM

Chapter 3

LIFESTYLE FOR A HEALTHY IMMUNE SYSTEM

One of the greatest benefits a "healthy" lifestyle gives us on a day-to-day basis is keeping our immune system balanced and strong. It is interesting to note that healthy living not only helps longevity but also has short-term rewards. While on the one hand it may keep us from heart disease, cancer, and other chronic ailments, in the short term it maximizes our bodies' protection from colds and flu. Researchers are finding proper nutrition, exercise, weight management, coping with stress, as well as taking certain vitamins and supplements all enhance immune system health—and we need a healthy immune system more today than ever before.

This is because there are more and more diseases being imported from various parts of the world and more that are growing resistant to our treatments. Not long ago the West Nile virus rolled through the United States causing problems for many. Severe acute respiratory syndrome (SARS) changed Chinese lifestyles as they donned masks and took other precautions to stop its spread. It also prompted caution around the rest of the world as cases cropped up among travelers, and with good reason: it appeared to be killing one out of every twenty-five who contracted it.

On the other hand, diseases such as staphylococcal (or staph) infections, which can be deadly for diabetics, and which we have normally been able to treat quite effectively with antibiotics, are developing resistance to those drugs and are again becoming a problem. Plus the fact that as antibiotics become more potent, they also kill more good bacteria that live in our intestines to help immune function and digestion. It is better to avoid these drugs because of this, but what is the alternative?

The only logical, long-term answer is that we develop an immune system that can deal with these infections and illnesses before they become a problem and need medication—and that begins with living a lifestyle that enhances rather than hinders our immune system response and function. That lifestyle begins with proper nutrition.

PROPER NUTRITION

As medicine turns more and more to prevention rather than cure, medical professionals are taking nutrition increasingly more seriously. One of the challenges with this, however, is to keep the nutritional plan simple enough to make it easy to follow. Often diet and nutrition books have long lists of do's and don'ts that are too difficult to remember and too difficult to follow regularly. On the other hand, some plans emphasize weight loss to the detriment of your health. The best plan is one that is healthy, low in bad fat, and high in fiber, while also being simple enough to adapt into your lifestyle—and I have had very few patients who have not been able to control their weight when they coupled such an eating pattern with regular exercise.

All of these are reasons why I have long been a proponent of what is called the Mediterranean diet. This is a diet that is low in red meats, hydrogenated oils, and processed foods (all major sources of bad fats and cholesterols), and high in fiber, nuts, fish, fruits, vegetables (especially salads), and olive oil (sources of good fats and cholesterols and other nutrients our bodies need)—all of which are also mentioned in the Bible and are the staples of dishes from Israel, Greece, Italy, and other nations that surround the Mediterranean Sea.

Two of the great benefits of the Mediterranean diet are that it emphasizes fruits rather than sweets and is lower in animal fats. Sugar and animal fat have both been shown to adversely affect the immune system. Sugar in particular, even honey, has been shown in tests to interfere with the ability of white blood cells to destroy bacteria. Soft drinks and other carbonated drinks have also been shown to decrease immune function, as has excessive alcohol consumption. Sticking to fruit juices, non-alcoholic red wines (or purple grape juice), and even simple water for our beverages is a great first step toward developing a more effective immune system.

THE MEDITERRANEAN DIET

By focusing on the Mediterranean diet as a guideline, it is easier to emphasize the do's so that the don'ts simply get left out. If we continually emphasize what not to eat, it seems like we are always living in denial, and mealtimes can become a legalistic regime of self-restraint. Yet just as in spiritual things, the question is not so much what not to do, but what to do. The Bible tells us to live in the Spirit and not by the flesh, meaning that a godly lifestyle is not so much a question of curbing the flesh as it is striving to live in the Spirit. "The law of the Spirit of life in Christ Jesus has set you free from the law of sin and of death" (Romans 8:2 NASB). By finding healthy foods that you like, it is always easier to let foods that are unhealthy fall out of your routine.

If you take a look at most Mediterranean menus, you will see that the following items make up most of what is eaten every day:

1. **Olive oil.** Excessive fat intake does impair immune system response to illnesses; however, the monounsaturated fats, such as those found in olive oil, do not appear to have this effect—in fact, these may even

strengthen the immune system. For this reason, olive oil is a great replacement for most fats, oils, butter, and margarine in our diet. Extra-virgin olive oil is preferred over other varieties.

2. **Breads.** Dark, chewy, high-fiber, crusty bread is present at most meals in the Mediterranean. Another good choice is Ezekiel bread, a recipe based on Ezekiel 4:9. Such high-fiber foods are a great help in reducing the effects of fat in our diet, and so are beneficial to our immune system. Typical American white bread made from processed white flours is not part of this diet.

3. **Pasta, rice, couscous, bulgur, potatoes.** Pasta is often served with fresh vegetables and herbs sautéed in olive oil; occasionally it is served with small quantities of lean beef. Tomato sauces that are often served with pasta are high in lycopene, one of the most potent antioxidants (substances that absorb or salvage harmful free radicals,

which damage cells and put a further strain on immune system function). Research done at the University of Milan showed that a three-week tomato-rich diet (60 grams of tomato puree daily) helped protect infection-fighting white blood cells.[1] Brown rice is preferred. Couscous and bulgur are other forms of whole grains.

4. **Grains.** To obtain the same healthy grains that are included from many different sources, eat cereals containing wheat bran (one-half cup, four to five times a week), or alternate with cereals such as Bran Buds (one-half cup) or those containing oat bran (one-third cup)—all of which contain water-soluble fibers. Eating this with soy milk rather than regular milk adds extra benefits because soy is a whole protein and thus reduces the need for red meat in the diet. If you have a soy allergy, use fat-free or low-fat milk.

5. **Fruits.** Several different fruits are available in the Mediterranean area, and they are usually eaten raw and at least two or three times a day. Since refined sugars inhibit immune function, fruits are a great replacement for sweets.

6. **Beans.** Include various kinds of beans in your diet: pinto, great northern, navy, lentil, kidney, etc. Bean and lentil soups are very popular in the Mediterranean countries and are usually prepared with a small amount of olive oil. You should have a half-cup or so of beans three or four times weekly.

7. **Nuts.** Ten unsalted almonds or walnuts a day have some wonderful benefits. Almonds in particular are higher in dietary fiber than most nuts, and are one of nature's best sources of amino acids and essential fatty acids, both of which are required for optimum immune system function.

8. **Vegetables and herbs.** Dark green vegetables are prominent in the Mediterranean diet, especially in salads. The updated food pyramid that has recently been appearing in science and news magazines suggests that vegetables should be eaten daily "in abundance." I suggest that you should eat at least one of the following cruciferous vegetables daily: cabbage, broccoli, cauliflower, turnip greens, or mustard greens (which are high in beta carotene and protect mucous membranes, especially in the lungs and intestinal tracts, from cancer and free-radical damage); and at least one from the following group of fruits and vegetables daily: carrots, spinach, sweet potatoes, cantaloupe, peaches, or apricots. More and more studies are showing that the equivalent of one clove of garlic a day (an herb used widely in the Mediterranean) can protect against free radicals, kill viruses responsible for colds and the flu, "rev up"

immune function by stimulating T cells, and also act as a decongestant. Eating more garlic can be a good defense if you feel a sore throat or cold coming on.

9. **Yogurt.** Eating fat-free, live-culture yogurt increases the body's production of infection-fighting gamma interferon. The live bacteria in yogurt (lactobacillus, streptococcus, and acidophilus) significantly strengthen the immune system (freezing yogurt to make a dessert kills these good bacteria). A light breakfast of one cup of fat-free yogurt with ten almonds and chopped fruit (particularly blueberries, strawberries, or raspberries) mixed with it is a great start to the day. In a UC–Davis study, subjects who ate yogurt daily in a yearlong test had 25 percent fewer colds than non-yogurt eaters.[2] Eating yogurt with your morning nutritional supplements also reduces the "vitamin taste" that can often linger after taking tablets and

capsules alone. Another low-fat, high-fiber breakfast alternative would be oatmeal or bran flakes with soy milk and fruit and six ounces of Concord grape or orange juice.

10. **Cheeses.** Mediterranean countries tend to eat lighter-colored dairy or white goat cheeses, usually grated or broken up on salads or in small wedges combined with fruit for a dessert. It is better to eat reduced- or low-fat cheeses (fat-free cheeses are often rubbery and not very palatable).

While all of these should be eaten daily, meats and proteins, on the other hand, should be eaten only a few times a week. I would put these in the following order of frequency and importance:

1. **Fish.** Cold-water fish high in omega-3 fatty acids such as cod, salmon, mackerel, and herring; trout is also good. Fish is the healthiest of meats that we can have in our diets. While studies have shown mixed

results of the effects of omega-3 fatty acids on the immune system, I still believe that these are the healthiest meat choices to gain the protein our bodies need and the benefits of these omega-3's to all the other systems of our bodies (such as the cardiovascular system).

2. **Poultry.** White breast meat without the skin is best. Poultry can be eaten two or three times a week.

3. **Eggs.** Eggs should be eaten no more than two or three times a week.

4. **Red meat.** The fat in red meat is the least desirable of all. When God spoke of not eating fat in Leviticus 3:17 and 7:23, I believe this is the type of fat He was talking about. The red meat eaten in Mediterranean countries tends to be much leaner and is eaten only two or three times a month. If you do include red meat in a meal, be sure to eat small portions of lean meat and trim whatever fat you can before you cook it.

While changing our diet is probably one of the more difficult on this list of things to do, it is also one of the most beneficial. Switching from the typical American diet of fatty red meat and processed starchy foods to one made up of salads, soups, whole grains, fruits and vegetables, and olive or canola oil is not only one of the healthiest things we can do, but also has the added benefit of helping us to eat and be satisfied while helping to control our weight.

OTHER FOODS BENEFICIAL TO IMMUNE SYSTEM BALANCE

SOY PRODUCTS. While the soybean is not typically part of the Mediterranean diet, it has several beneficial characteristics that make it worth mentioning here. First of all, it is an excellent protein substitute for red meat. You can receive whole proteins from the plant kingdom by combining certain vegetables (beans and rice or corn, for example), but it appears that soy is the only plant that is a complete protein in and of itself. In other words, it is the only plant that has all of the essential amino acids necessary for the formation of proteins in one package. Soy also contains isoflavones, or flavonoids (also called bioflavonoids), a major category of plant antioxidants.

Soy is now available in a variety of products from tofu to tempeh, soy ice cream, milk, yogurt, cheese, flour, and even roasted soy nuts. Tofu is perhaps the most popular form, and has no real flavor of its own, but absorbs flavor from whatever it is cooked with. It can easily be worked into a wide variety of recipes—from stir-fry to roasted and from frozen to marinade. Actually, my wife and I have never been able to work tofu into our diet because of its unusual texture. I encourage you to at least try it, but we understand if you choose another way to get the benefits of soy!

The way we have worked around this is to drink soymilk. We regularly have soymilk on our breakfast cereal—we started with vanilla soymilk, and have found a variety of others that we like including chocolate and "creamy" (this is not mixed with cream, but thickened with other natural proteins).

POMEGRANATES. Recent studies have been presented showing that pomegranate seed oil and juice can have beneficial effects. Two studies represented at an international conference in June 2001 indicated that pomegranate seed oil triggered apoptosis—a self-destruct mechanism, if you will—in breast cancer cells, while having no adverse effects on healthy breast cells.[3] Another study in the *American Journal of Clinical Nutrition* indicated that pomegranate juice consumption reduced oxidative stress and contributed to cardiovascular health.[4] Fresh and dried pomegranate seeds are used widely in Indian and Thai recipes as a seasoning.

MAITAKE, REISHI, AND SHIITAKE MUSHROOMS. We're all familiar with the culinary uses for mushrooms, but did you know that several varieties have benefits that go beyond taste and texture? Studies from Baylor College of Medicine and M. D. Anderson Cancer Center in Houston have shown the health benefits of mushrooms on the immune system. In particular, maitake, reishi, and shiitake mushrooms, which can be found at your local market or specialty grocery store, or obtained in extract form, have been shown to help balance the immune system and even fight cancer.

Maitake has been called "King of the Mushrooms." Research shows that it inhibits tumors and stimulates a weakened immune system. In fact, in a large study in China, it actually fought and killed cancer cells associated with lung, stomach, and liver cancer.[5]

The reishi mushroom's primary effect is with allergies. Polysaccharide compounds (beta 1, 3 glucan) in the reishi mushroom actually balance an overactive immune system so that it doesn't attack things that are harmless to the body. In other words, it helps treat allergies by inhibiting histamine release, and thereby alleviates allergy symptoms. For pennies, you can use extracts from this type of mushroom as compared to dollars a pill for prescription medications to treat these bothersome symptoms of allergies.

Shiitake has an unusual and extremely potent compound in it called *lentinan*. Studies have shown lentinan to be so effective in stabilizing the immune system that it is currently being studied as a possible treatment for the HIV-AIDS infection.[6] Lentinan also appears to be very good at eliminating and fighting cancer.

While these mushrooms are great foods to add to your diet for their benefits, it is tough to eat them every day. They are so valuable, though, that many are creating supplements containing extracts from them so that you can take them with your regular basic daily vitamin and nutritional supplement program. More and more evidence is being published to indicate that proper nutrition may no longer be possible without adding vitamins and supplements to your diet on a daily basis. Because of the importance of the topic of nutritional supplements, we will discuss it in more detail in the next chapter.

AVOID FOODS THAT STIMULATE THE IMMUNE SYSTEM IF YOU ARE FACING AUTOIMMUNE DISEASE

As we have discussed briefly before, if you are facing autoimmune diseases such as lupus, rheumatoid arthritis, or polymyositis, it is because of an overactive immune system. In such cases it is best to avoid foods that increase immune system function and sensitivity such as the following:

ALFALFA SPROUTS. There is a chemical in alfalfa sprouts, *l-canavanine,* that increases the immune system's attack on the kidneys, heart, joints, and skin. This is extremely bad for those suffering from lupus, because these organs are the main ones attacked by this disease. Rheumatoid arthritis sufferers should also avoid this vegetable because of the enhanced attack on the joints.

SHELLFISH AND ZINC. All of us can benefit from 15 milligrams a day of zinc, but larger quantities ranging from 50 to 100 milligrams a day should be avoided by autoimmune disease sufferers. Zinc will aggravate the immune system's attack on the body.

Though we normally advise against eating shellfish for a number of reasons, those who have lupus or other autoimmune disease should be even more careful about eating it, as it normally has high quantities of zinc.

CORN, SAFFLOWER, AND SUNFLOWER OILS. These oils contain omega-6 fatty acids, which also stimulate and worsen autoimmune diseases. There are also indications that these may also increase the risks of breast and colon cancer. These are quite different from the omega-

3 fatty acids found in fish, which can actually help alleviate some of the inflammation that is another result of an overactive immune system.

EXERCISE

Our modern sedentary lifestyles have some tremendous drawbacks for our general health. Jesus never had to tell His disciples they needed exercise because they walked everywhere they went, from city to city and region to region. Such exercise is not a regular part of our modern culture, however, and therefore we have to work at getting enough exercise into our weekly routines.

When I talk about getting enough exercise, I am actually talking about something as simple as walking forty to forty-five minutes, three to five times a week, or you can break this down further to a brisk walk every day for about 20 minutes. This is enough to get your heart rate up, get your muscles working and pumping, and doesn't require an expensive membership to a health club. Obviously you could do more (it is even advisable to start with less if you find this too challenging), but I have always believed in starting with simple changes, and then working your way forward as God leads you. It is also important not to start with too much activity, since that can stress your system more than help.

Walking, jogging, stationary cycling, outdoor cycling, water exercise, tennis, stretching, aerobic classes, and swimming are all fine workouts. The important thing is to find something you enjoy and will do regularly to build your aerobic capacity. As you improve your fitness, you can combine various forms of exercise to address all your different muscle groups and body systems. Remember to do proper warm-ups and cool-downs. It is also better to eat after exercising rather than before, as the exercise will contribute to food absorption and burning calories.

Such regular activity has great benefits for your immune system. Research has indicated, for example, that subjects who do moderate exercise as part of their weekly routine have fewer upper respiratory infections (coughs, colds, and the flu)—however those who over-taxed their bodies through exercise actually had more.[7]

The lymph system is central to the proper immune response function, and is a system that is even more intricate than the cardiovascular system, yet has no pump, or heart, as the cardiovascular system does. Instead, it relies on the movement of the muscles and body to help it flow. For this reason regular exercise and stretching seem to have a positive effect on keeping this system fit and responsive. Regular exercise has also been shown to help cope with stress, which seems to reduce immune system effectiveness (we will discuss this in more detail in the section on "Coping With Stress and Grief").

DETERMINE YOUR SAFE HEART-RATE RANGE

Whatever exercise you choose, you should work at it vigorously enough to get your heart rate elevated during the time you are exercising. Physical fitness experts have a simple formula for determining a safe heart-rate range for exercising. Simply subtract your age from 220 to find your maximum heart rate. Say you are forty years old: your formula would be 220–40 = 180. Your target heart-rate zone is between 60 and 80 percent of that number. So multiply your maximum heart rate by 0.6 for the bottom of your safe exercise range and by 0.8 for the top. As you exercise, check your pulse rate now and then, and be sure your heartbeat is within that range. So for the example above, the safe heart range for a forty-year-old would be 108 to 144.

Find your pulse in your wrist or neck, count the number of beats in ten seconds, and multiply that number by six. If the number you get is within your safe exercise range, you're fine. If it's lower, work harder. If it's higher, slow down a little. When starting an exercise program, aim at the lowest part of your target zone for the first few weeks, then you can gradually build up to the higher part of your target zone.

WEIGHT MANAGEMENT

Both being underweight and overweight are associated with lower immune system response and effectiveness, while obesity (defined as being thirty or more pounds overweight) has been associated with increased risk of infection for hospitalized patients. However, dietary restrictions or certain "fad" diet plans seem to be equally detrimental to immune function. Regular aerobic exercise alone has been shown to offset the detrimental effects of both excessive weight and weight-loss diets.[8]

My recommendation is to avoid diets strictly aimed at weight loss, because they are seldom effective, and when they are, the weight is just as often put back on again when the person goes off the diet. Some of the more popular weight-loss diets today are even unhealthy. I believe it is best to adapt a moderate, low-fat, high-fiber meal plan or diet *for life* such as the Mediterranean diet, and then to add regular moderate exercise to that. This combination has been great to maintain health as well as control weight for many of my patients.

COPING WITH STRESS AND GRIEF

Have you ever noticed that you get sick right in the midst of or right after a time of intense stress? A big project at the office closes; you just finished the cleanup after your child's wedding; you lost your job; there was a death in the family; you just moved to another house. Times of intense stress or grief are hard on your immune system and more often than not open you up to infections or more serious ailments if they persist over time. No wonder the Bible tells us: "The joy of the LORD is your strength" (Nehemiah 8:10), and "A merry heart does good, like medicine, but a broken spirit dries the bones" (Proverbs 17:22 NKJV).

Jesus warned us several times that we would face various trials and temptations in this life. I would classify these as times of stress, wouldn't you? But He said He would always be with us in the midst of them. Because of this, we know we can lean on Him in the spiritual realm and never let go of our joy regardless of the circumstances. Such a great spiritual revelation has wonderful natural consequences to our health.

At the same time we can also do things in the natural to help us better deal with times of stress, trial, and grief. Anything you do to your body you are also doing to your immune system. Going without sleep, working long hours, or worrying excessively taxes our immune system and makes it less able to respond. Not eating nutritiously, not exercising regularly, and not taking our nutritional supplements all limit our bodies' natural ability to deal with stress. We need to spend time developing ourselves spirit, soul, and body just as we need to spend time developing our family, social, professional, financial, and church lives. A balanced lifestyle is a great help in maintaining a balanced immune system and limiting the effects of stress on our lives.

GOD'S PLAN FOR HEALTHY LIVING

The fruits of the spirit are not in our lives just to please God—although they do please Him. He has also added with them the blessing of a long, healthy life. Love, joy, peace, patience, kindness, goodness, faithfulness, gentleness, and self-control (see Galatians 5:22–23 NKJV) are manifestations of the Spirit God wants to see in our lives in abundance, because they bring with them good health and success.

There are reasons why the self-indulgence and lack of discipline that lead to poor eating habits, being overweight, and not getting enough exercise are not on this list, because they wreak havoc on our immune system and therefore our health, among many other things.

Isn't it amazing to think that we can handle so many different diseases by taking care of this one system of our body? God made it simple to understand and has outlined it clearly for us in His Word. He is also going the extra step by revealing to us in these latter days the things that we need to know to stay healthy. He is revealing to us through medical science and through ministries such as ours the natural compounds that He provided in His creation for our health. As He blesses our food and water (all that we eat and drink) He will keep sickness from the midst of us (see Exodus 23:25–26), and in the leaves of the trees He has provided compounds for the healing of the nations (see Revelation 22:2). He has provided us with a balanced attack of supernatural healing power and natural healing wisdom to show us the pathway to healing He has for any illness we may face. It is up to us to heed His instructions and put His plan of healthy living into action.

We must build a balanced lifestyle as a basis for a balanced immune system, but God has also provided other elements and natural compounds to help us in this as we face things that even our balanced lifestyle cannot handle. People with strong immune systems still get sick when they face a virus or bacteria that their systems have never conquered before, but an immune system that responds quickly can eliminate such unwanted visitors much faster than a weak one. For this reason, in the following chapters we will look at some of the natural compounds and nutritional supplements that can also help us to maintain a strong and responsive immune system so that we can stay healthy or recover from illness more quickly.

Chapter 4

VITAMINS AND SUPPLEMENTS FOR IMMUNE SYSTEM SUPPORT

Chapter 4

VITAMINS AND SUPPLEMENTS FOR IMMUNE SYSTEM SUPPORT

In a *Journal of the American Medical Association* article entitled "The Graying of the Immune System," immune system expert Ranjit Chandra discussed how immune response tends to slow in most people as we age. As we reach the age of fifty-five to sixty we tend to have reduced immune system function because of lower interleukin-2 production, decreased lymphocyte response to antigens, and a decreased concentration of antibodies that form after vaccination. However, in some elderly people, the immune system seems to be just as active as it was when they were much younger. Nutrition seems to be a major key in the difference between these two groups, and this nutrition is connected to regular vitamin and supplement intake rather than through meals and diet alone. In fact, the article cited that "Nutrition is a critical determinant of immunocompetence in all age groups, including the elderly." Dr. Chandra concluded, "The era of nutrient supplements to promote health and reduce illness is here to stay. In selected groups such as the elderly, there is overwhelming evidence of immunologic enhancement following such an intervention."[1]

In a study reported in *Internal Medicine News,* researchers gave either a daily multivitamin/mineral supplement or a placebo to ninety-six elderly individuals for one year. They found that subjects on supplements had increased antibody responses and significantly higher numbers of T cells and NK cells than before. This group also averaged roughly twenty-three "sick days" a year compared to forty-eight sick days in the placebo group.[2]

In addition to this, in a June 2002 article, the American Medical Association began recommending multivitamins for all Americans for the first time ever. Their recommendation was that all adults take a daily multivitamin and that elderly adults take two a day (seeing, of course, that they do not get more than the daily-recommended allowance of vitamins such as Vitamin A, which can be toxic if taken in too high a dosage for too long).[3]

Typically we all have a slow decrease of immune function that begins in our late twenties and thirties and becomes significantly noticeable by our late fifties. Research is showing more and more that daily vitamins, minerals, and other nutritional supplements are tremendously beneficial in countering this trend by strengthening the immune system in its efforts to fight disease and chronic illness. In addition to the lifestyle factors that strengthen the immune system, discussed in the last chapter, all of us should be on some form of basic daily nutritional supplement program. Those of us who are getting older or have other immune system challenges should also consider adding to that daily routine compounds that will more specifically balance and fortify immune response.

BASIC NUTRITIONAL SUPPORT

Because of our fast, fatty, and processed food diets as well as the depletion of nutrients in our fruits, vegetables, and livestock because of the effort to produce quantity rather than quality foods, we cannot look solely to our diets to get the nutrition we need to stay healthy. The best answer to this at present seems to be taking nutritional supplements containing vitamins, minerals, extracts, enzymes, bioflavonoids, and marine oils every day with our meals. While there are a variety of options open to us in what we can take every day, without the correct information it is possible that we are not getting enough of what we need or are getting too much. Because of the depth of this subject, there is not space enough in this book to cover it adequately, but you can get further information on this topic from my book *God's Pathway to Healing: Vitamins and Supplements,* or visit our Web site at *www. abundantnutrition.com.*

OTHER VITAMINS AND SUPPLEMENTS FOR IMMUNE SYSTEM HEALTH

In addition to a daily nutritional support program, there are several vitamins, minerals, herbs, and extracts that specifically benefit immune response and function.

VITAMINS

Vitamins A, C, and E, usually grouped together because of their antioxidant qualities, increase the number of lymphocytes in our body as well as enhance lymphocyte response to antigens. Their antioxidant qualities also help the immune system by eliminating free radicals—renegade half-oxygen molecules that can damage or "tear" cells in our bodies as they look to find the additional electrons to complete themselves. This process makes other cells "sick" or turns them cancerous and requires the immune system to eliminate them altogether. By reducing this need to repair free-radical damage, the immune system can pay more attention to antigens.

VITAMIN E. Vitamin E seems especially helpful in enhancing lymphocyte response to antigens. I recommend that you take 800 international units (IU) of this daily, which is an amount already present in many daily nutritional supplement plans. Be careful to avoid higher amounts, as it begins to weaken the immune system when you get in the range of 1,500 IU a day.

VITAMIN C. Vitamin C contributes greatly to the production of T cells and other immune system agents as well as being critical for lymphocyte function. I recommend 2,000 milligrams a day of vitamin C for this and other benefits.

VITAMIN A (FROM BETA CAROTENE). I generally don't recommend taking vitamin A in its own form, but instead recommend taking beta carotene, which is another antioxidant, and which the body uses to create vitamin A. Thus, I recommend 2,500 IU of beta carotene daily to handle your vitamin A requirements while decreasing the risk of getting too much vitamin A, which can interfere with liver function, cause dry and cracking skin, brittle nails and bones, and bleeding gums. By taking it in beta carotene form, your body only produces the vitamin A you need.

MINERALS

COPPER. This essential mineral is needed for the synthesis of connective tissue and for proper immune function. Studies indicate that marginal copper deficiency can significantly increase the risk of colon cancer. Copper appears to be a strong stimulant of white blood cells, from which most of the immune system's agents, such as lymphocytes and phagocytes, are formed. I recommend 500 micrograms of it daily to help an imbalanced immune system.

SELENIUM. In one study 1,300 people took 200 micrograms of selenium daily. It cut the rate of all cancers in this population by over 40 percent, and cut lung, prostate, and colon cancers by 50 percent![4] Selenium stimulates the NK or "Natural Killer" cells of the immune system, which hone in on cancerous cells and eliminate them. But selenium doesn't only act to stimulate the immune system, it also balances it.

Though it increases the number of NK and T cells and their function, it also reduces the number of overactive antibodies in the thyroid (which can cause thyroiditis, an autoimmune disease that attacks the thyroid) and therefore improves thyroid function. One study of seventy-two women with low thyroid function were given selenium to see how it would affect them. It decreased these anti-thyroid antibodies and markedly improved thyroid function in most of the women.

ZINC. You should take 15 milligrams a day with a possible additional 10 milligrams a day if you have a weakened immune system. More than this, starting at around 50 milligrams of zinc a day, actually starts interfering with the immune system. Normally your body needs roughly a 10 to 1 copper to zinc ratio for optimal health.

HERBS

ASTRAGALUS. Studies have shown that 100 milligrams of astragalus root extract a day increases T cell and T helper cell counts. The T helper cell is actually an immune system mobile command center that literally directs NK cell functions and other immune system agents and activities. Astragalus is one of the most important things you can take to balance the immune system—if it is weak, it strengthens it; but if it is overactive, by producing more T helper cells it helps to regulate it. This is very critical to battle respiratory infections and to overcome the typical age-related decline of immune function. I generally recommend 50 milligrams of this herb on a daily basis.

GARLIC. We already discussed the benefits of garlic in the previous chapter's section on the Mediterranean diet, but I also wanted to point out that this herb is available in extract form as well. Researchers have found thirty different cancer-fighting compounds in garlic alone that positively affect multiple body systems, most important of which are the cardiovascular and immune systems. One hundred milligrams a day of garlic bulb extract can significantly help your immune system's function.

OTHER EXTRACTS AND COMPOUNDS

BLUEBERRIES. Blueberries are one of the most potent sources of antioxidants and bioflavonoids that can be found. They also do a great job of maintaining the integrity of the body's connective tissues. Since they are somewhat seasonal and can be expensive in the off-season, it is best to include them in our supplements in powder or extract form. I suggest 75 milligrams of this extract a day.

ELDERBERRIES. While the bitterness of elderberries often keeps them from being used in anything but pies and jams, they have been shown in studies to cut flu symptoms by 50 percent because they directly inhibit viruses and stimulate immune response.[6] Because of these findings, I suggest taking elderberry extract in dosages of 50 milligrams a day.

POMEGRANATE SEED. We already discussed the help that pomegranates can have in eliminating breast cancer cells in the previous section on "Other Foods Beneficial to Immune System Balance." It is good to know that, as with other fruits, pomegranate seed extract can be added to your daily nutritional supplements to maximize its benefits. I recommend 25 milligrams of this extract daily.

MUSHROOMS. All three forms of the mushrooms we discussed in the "Other Foods Beneficial to Immune System Balance" of the previous chapter can also be taken in extract form in order to receive their full benefits on a more regular basis. I generally suggest 25 milligrams a day of maitake extract, and 5 milligrams a day of each of the other two: reishi and shiitake.

Another valuable mushroom extract is that of the cordyceps sinensis mushroom. It has been used for centuries in China to increase energy, endurance, and stamina. In fact, in 1993 it received a good deal of attention when Chinese Olympic swimmers took this supplement as part of their training program and set world records in several events. Studies among the elderly with cordyceps showed that it helped subjects get relief from the symptoms of fatigue that they may have been experiencing as well as better tolerate cold, especially in their hands and feet. Its efficiency rate for relieving these symptoms was somewhere between 80 and 90 percent. A more recent study by the American College of Sports Medicine found that this compound increased the oxygen intake of the body, which is how it improves energy and endurance and thus athletic performance and resistance to fatigue.[7]

BETA 1, 3 GLUCAN. We have already discussed the benefits of this compound, which is found in reishi mushrooms. It is a polysaccharide compound, a complex carbohydrate actually, and is also found in common baker's yeast, although it is found there in a slightly different form, and can now be taken in a supplement, as well. It is also similar to the polysaccharide compound found in aloe vera. I generally recommend 25 milligrams of this extract daily for a weakened immune system.

One of the big benefits of this compound, as we discussed before, is in the treatment of allergies. Beta 1, 3 glucan (also called simply "beta glucan") has the unique ability to strengthen a weakened immune system, but also to curb its overstimulation, which is what causes allergies. A study reported in the *Archives of Surgery,* found that beta 1, 3 glucan also decreased the incidence and rate of post-operative infections. It seems to specifically help the macrophages ("big eater" cells), which engulf pathogens to keep the antigens they may be carrying from causing infections.[8]

LACTOBACILLUS SPOROGENES. This is actually a bacteria that is very stable in capsule form and is important for immune health in the gastrointestinal tract. This good bacteria helps eliminate antigens primarily in the large intestines, but is being wiped out by the antibiotics we ingest from the factory-farmed meats we eat—specifically from chicken. Such farms generally pump their animals full of antibiotics on a regular basis to keep them healthy, and then those drugs are passed on to us when we eat them. Thus, the best way to counteract this is to take more good bacteria in capsule form to replenish our systems. I recommend 25 milligrams a day of this form of good bacteria to keep the immune system strong.

ARABINIGALACTAN. This herbal compound comes from the larch tree and technically is classified as a prebiotic, which means it has an enhancing effect on the friendly bacteria that dwell inside the human GI tract. It enhances immune cell function (those cells lining the intestinal tract), it increases a component of the immune system known as killer cells, and some studies show it can even stop the metastases, or spread, of cancer cells.

GLUCONO-DELTA-LACTONE. This compound also feeds and promotes normal function of the friendly bacteria in the GI tract. It is a carbohydrate derivative and helps create a barrier against the bad bacteria that might invade the body through the lining of the intestinal tract. It also assists in recolonizing the GI tract with good bacteria following the use of antibiotics.

L-GLUTAMINE. L-Glutamine is an amino acid that is used as an energy source for immune cells. This compound is naturally produced in the muscles of the body and is transported by blood to the cells. This also enhances the ability of the intestinal lining to resist invasions by harmful microorganisms.

INULIN. Inulin is also classified as a prebiotic, increasing the friendly flora in the GI tract. It helps prevent bacteria as well as virus and yeast from adhering to the wall of the GI tract, and it is a natural-occurring fiberlike substance.

OLIVE LEAF EXTRACT. Olive leaf extract has a direct effect on bacteria (which we call an antimicrobial effect). This herbal derivative essentially hinders the growth of harmful microorganisms.

SIBERIAN GINSENG ROOT EXTRACT (ELEUTHEROCOCCUS). This herb has a long history of increasing a component of the immune system known as T lymphocytes, and it has been used for centuries to increase resistance to stress, fatigue, and illness.

ECHINACEA AND GOLDENSEAL ARE BEST USED SHORT-TERM

Echinacea and goldenseal are great herbs to use for short periods of time to help you get over a cold or flu, but there are concerns about their long-term use. Most herbalists do not recommend taking Echinacea for more than a few weeks because the effectiveness of the herb tends to diminish over time. Some researchers even believe that Echinacea can actually suppress the immune system when used for longer than a month or two. Since it stimulates immune system response, it can even be harmful if you are suffering from autoimmune diseases such as lupus, rheumatoid arthritis, or chronic fatigue syndrome.

Some people report gastric upset when they use goldenseal on a daily basis, because it can irritate the sensitive lining of the stomach. It is also dangerous to take goldenseal during pregnancy as it can cause premature contractions and induce a miscarriage. Because of these concerns, I do not recommend taking them regularly, though they can be good to have in your medicine cabinet to help combat colds, coughs, and flu.

WE ALL NEED A BALANCED AND HEALTHY IMMUNE SYSTEM

Balancing an immune system that may not be reacting properly is crucial to staying healthy and fighting disease. By taking the right combination of prominent vitamins and minerals, along with other proven fruit and plant extracts, you can keep your immune system in balance and reap the health benefits that God intended for all of us.

Chapter 5

YOUR DAILY WALK ON THE PATHWAY TO A HEALTHY AND VIBRANT IMMUNE SYSTEM

Chapter 5

YOUR DAILY WALK ON THE PATHWAY TO A HEALTHY AND VIBRANT IMMUNE SYSTEM

Those who live in the shelter of the Most
   High will find rest in the shadow of
   the Almighty.

This I declare of the LORD:
He alone is my refuge, my place of safety;
   he is my God, and I am trusting him.

For he will rescue you from every trap
and protect you from the fatal plague.

He will shield you with his wings.
He will shelter you with his feathers.
His faithful promises are your armor and
    protection. . . .

If you make the LORD your refuge,
if you make the Most High your shelter,
no evil will conquer you;
no plague will come near your dwelling.

For he orders his angels
to protect you wherever you go.
(Psalm 91:1–4, 9–11 NLT)

The immune system has always seemed to
me to be the natural equivalent of the spiritual
principles of protection found in Psalm 91—it
is the body's shield and defense against disease,
just as God is our place of refuge against calam-
ity and attack. Just as His angels will protect us
wherever we go, so the agents of the immune
system protect from whatever invader might
attack us physically. This is why I say that in
the immune system we see the hand of God

reaching down to heal us; it has the fingerprints of His creative and healing power all over it.

In this parallel I believe we also see the pattern of how God wants us to operate in our lives—by balancing spiritual principles with natural wisdom to direct our steps. Because of this I have developed five steps to keep this balance in our lives and make sure we are either following God's plan for healthy living or finding His pathway to healing for whatever health challenges we may be facing.

Step 1: Consult with a physician or reliable medical professional. Make sure you have regular checkups to catch potential problems early when they are easiest to treat and correct. Many say that they don't need to go to doctors because they are doing all the things they need to do in order to maintain their health. I believe this is often fear speaking more than wisdom. Having regular checkups not only keeps you from unnecessary worry about your health, but also gives you the chance to discuss immune system balancing strategies with your health professional.

Consultation with a physician or a competent medical professional can give you information about your health and immune system that is vital. As I have said before, it is often the only opportunity to catch health problems while they are still simple to treat. Be sure to discuss with your health advisor all the different supplements you may be taking to ensure there are no conflicts. This person may even be able to suggest a packaged supplement program that contains all or most of what you need to take on a daily basis, making nutritional supplementation even easier. You should also discuss your diet and exercise programs with your doctor or advisor to see if he or she has any other advice that might be helpful in these areas.

Step 2: Pray with understanding. Seek God in prayer and ask Him to reveal to you and to your doctor the best steps in the natural that you can take to proceed down your pathway to maintaining your health or receiving your healing.

While much of the advice I have offered in this pocket book is practical, do not neglect your daily spiritual needs. Make sure to "supplement" what you take into your mind and body every day with solid doses of God's Word and prayer. Only then can God lead you into the fullness and abundance of life He has promised you in all areas.

If you are not sure how to pray for your immune system, you can begin by praying a prayer like the following for yourself or for your loved ones:

Father, I thank you in the name of Jesus that my immune system is strong and balanced. I thank you, Father, that according to Leviticus 17:11, "The life of the flesh is in the blood," and that life will continue to flow to every cell in my body. I thank you that my lymphocytes, T cells, NK cells,

B cells, antibodies, and other immune agents are strong and responsive to invading antigens, and that any disease that enters my body will not have time to create symptoms before it is eliminated. Cancer will not have a chance to spread, and tumors will not be able to form, because you have blessed my system with strength and responsiveness.

I also thank you that my immune system "has glasses on" and knows what to attack and what to leave alone. I thank you that my immune system will not be overactive, and that allergies and autoimmune disease will be far from me.

Quicken to me the things I should do to change my lifestyle and eating habits to keep my immune system strong, and help me to cultivate the fruit of self-control to make these habits part of my normal routine. Guide me as I develop a daily nutritional supplement program so that I get the nutrients I need most to remain a strong and healthy light for you in everything I do. I will be obedient to the guiding of the Holy Spirit.

Thank you, Father, for setting me free from sickness and disease as you bless what I eat and drink, and that I will fulfill the number of my days according to your promises.

In Jesus' name I pray. Amen.

Step 3: Ask the Holy Spirit to guide you to truth. I have given you a great deal of information about things you can do or take to help your physical body, and it is quite possible that your medical advisor will give you some other options. By referring to the information in this book, you can bring up the discussion of what would be best for you. Approach your health professional by asking if he or she would be willing to work with you in developing a nutritional supplement program or whether they can suggest other steps for you to keep your immune system functioning at its optimal level.

I strongly encourage you to explore all the aspects of immune system health that I have shared with you in this pocket book—the pathways that God has created to strengthen and guard your body. You need to pray in faith that God will give you the wisdom you need in order to discern the one pathway He has provided that is best for you. James 1:5 gives us God's promise about receiving this wisdom: "If any of you lack wisdom, let him ask of God, that giveth to all men liberally, and upbraideth not; and it shall be given him." Allow the Holy Spirit to guide you to all truth.

Step 4: Maintain proper and healthy nutrition. Exercise your body and mind to stay fit. In other words, dedicate yourself to living the immune-healthy lifestyle I have outlined in chapter 3. Make these things a regular part of your routine, and remember to make them fun and not a burden. Find a variety of foods and recipes that you like that are part of the Mediterranean diet and experiment with these healthy, natural ingredients to create your own delicious meals. Find an exercise program you enjoy. While some may enjoy walking on a treadmill while watching television, others will need to get outside or find a competitive sport to challenge them, or a group activity to socially encourage them. Don't let it become drudgery, or you won't keep it up over time.

Studies have shown that we also need to challenge ourselves intellectually to maintain healthier mental faculties. Establish an active lifestyle for an active body and mind.

Step 5: Stand firm in God's pathway to healing for you. Refuse to be discouraged or defeated. Be aggressive in prayer and in faith, claiming your health and healing in Jesus Christ.

GOD HAS A UNIQUE PATHWAY TO HEALTH FOR YOU

There are nineteen individually recorded healings in the Gospels, and each is unique in its own way. I believe these are all recorded in the Scriptures to show us that God uses different methods to deliver His healing power. When I realized this, it completely changed the way I practiced medicine. It is incredible how when I started praying and asking God to show me, as a doctor, His pathway to healing for each of my patients, I began to see more and more clearly His design for helping each person. Through prayer, faith, knowledge, and wisdom, God can show you His pathway to maintaining health or to receiving healing.

If we are open to that, God will work miracles. It may be instantaneous, or it may be a process or treatment that takes some time. Just as many chronic diseases take time to develop, they will also take time to reverse. It may involve certain prescription medications, or even surgery. It could also be a pathway that is relatively uneventful as we maintain our health through regular checkups. Thank God that we can pray for our healing, but also that we can take precautions before we are sick to avoid the need for healing. Either way, we have tremendous hope.

Hebrews 11:1 says that faith gives substance to those things we hope for. But if you don't have anything to hope for, how will faith give substance to it? You have to have hope, and that hope comes when you know that God has a pathway to health or healing for you. That is a promise you can hold on to, pray for, and have faith in. Thank God for His promises!

These are principles to apply in all areas of your life, but you can specifically apply them with regard to your immune system health. Seek God specifically in the areas you have concerns about and find His answers. See a physician to get the right information so that you know specifically how to pray. God knows your needs as well as the best way for you to receive your healing and maintain your health. Hang on to the hope of His promises, and He will show you His plan for healthy living that is especially designed for you.

ENDNOTES

Chapter 3

1. Patrizia Riso, Andrew Pinder, Alessandra Santangelo, and Marisa Porrini, "Does Tomato Consumption Effectively Increase the Resistance of Lymphocyte DNA to Oxidate Damage?" *American Journal of Clinical Nutrition* 69:4 (April 1999): 712-18.
2. J. Van de Water, C. L. Keen, H. E. Gershwin, "The Influence of Chronic Yogurt Consumption on Immunity," *Journal of Nutrition* 129 (1999): 14925–53.
3. PR Newswire, "Studies Show Pomegranate Seed Oil Causes Breast Cancer Cells to Self-Destruct," online at *http://workgroups.newsedge.com/display_p.asp?doc_id=NEp0820051.100*. Created: 21 August 2001. Accessed: 21 August 2001.

4. Michael Aviram, Leslie Dornfeld, et al., "Pomegranate Juice Consumption Reduces Oxidative Stress, Atherogenic Modifications to LDL, and Platelet Aggression: Studies in Humans and in Atherosclerotic Apolipoprotein E-Deficient Mice," *American Journal of Clinical Nutrition* 71:5 (May 2000): 1062–76.

5. Y. Yamada, H. Nanba, H. Kuroda, "Antitumor Effect of Orally Administered Extracts From Fruit Body of *Grifola Frondosa*" [maitake], *Chemotherapy* 38 (1990): 790–96.

6. *www.diet-and-health.net/Naturopathy/Shiitake.html.*

7. D. C. Nieman, "Exercise and Resistance to Infection," *Canadian Journal of Physiology and Pharmacology* 76:5 (May 1998): 573–80 [Review].

8. Healthwell.com, "Immune Function," online at: *www.healthwell.com/Healthnotes/Concern/Immune_Function.cfm?path=hw.* Last updated: 2 August 1999. Accessed: 29 April 2003.

Chapter 4

1. Ranjit Kumar Chandra, OC, MD, FRCPC, "The Graying of the Immune System," *Journal*

of the American Medical Association 277:17 (7 May 1997): 1398–99 [Commentary].

2. *Lancet,* 340:7 (1992): 1124–27.

3. Robert H. Fletcherm, M.D., M.Sc.; and Kathleen M. Farfield, M.D., Ph.D; "Vitamins for Chronic Disease Prevention in Adults: Clinical Applications," *The Journal of the American Medical Association* 287:23 (19 June 2002): 3129.

4. L. C. Clark, G. F. J. Combs, B. W. Turnbull, et al., "Effects of Selenium Supplementation for Cancer Prevention in Patients With Carcinoma of the Skin." Published erratum appears in *JAMA* (May 21, 1997): 277.

5. M. Gordon, B. Bihari, E. Goosby, et al., "A Placebo-Controlled Trial of the Immune Modulator, Lentinan, in HIV-Positive Patients: A Phase I/II Trial," *Journal of Medicine* 29:5–6 (1998): 305-30.

6. Z. Zakay-Rones, N. Varsano, M. Zlotnik, et al., "Inhibition of Several Strains of Influenza Virus in Vitro and Reduction of Symptoms by an Elderberry Extract (Sambucus Nigra L.) During an Outbreak of Influenza B Panama,"

J. Altern Complement Med., 1995; 1:361–369.

7. Y. Xiao, X. Z. Huang, G. Chen, et al., "Increased Aerobic Capacity in Healthy Elderly Human Adults Given a Fermentation Product of Cordyceps Cs–4," *Medicine and Science in Sports and Exercise* S174 (1999): 31.

8. T. J. Babineau, et al., "A Phase II Multicenter Double-Blind Randomized Placebo-Controlled Study of Three Dosages of an Immunuomodulator (PGB-glucan) in High-Risk Surgical Patients," *Archives of Surgery* 120 (1994): 1204–10.

REGINALD B. CHERRY, M.D.—A MEDICAL DOCTOR'S TESTIMONY

The first six years of my life were lived in the dusty rural town of Mansfield, in the Ouachita Mountains of western Arkansas. In those childhood years, I had one seemingly impossible dream—to become a doctor!

Through God's grace, I graduated from Baylor University and the University of Texas Medical School. Throughout those years, I felt God tug on my heart a number of times, especially through Billy Graham, as I heard him preach on TV. But I never surrendered my life to Jesus Christ.

In those early days of practicing medicine, I

met Dr. Kenneth Cooper and became trained in the field of preventive medicine. In the mid-seventies I moved to Houston and established a medical practice for preventive medicine. Sadly, at that time money became a driving force in my life.

Nevertheless, God was looking out for me. He brought into our clinic a nurse who became a Spirit-filled Christian, and she began praying for me. In fact, she had her whole church praying for me!

In my search for fulfillment and meaning in life, I called out to God one night in late November 1979 and prayed, *Jesus, I give you everything I own. I'm sorry for the life I've lived. I want to live for you the rest of my days. I give you my life.* A doctor had been born again, and that beautiful nurse, Linda, who had prayed for me and shared Jesus with me, is now my wife!

Not only did Jesus transform my life but He also transformed my medical practice. God spoke to me and said in effect, "I want you to establish a Christian clinic. From now on when you practice medicine, you will be *ministering* to patients." I began to pray for patients seeking God's pathway to healing in the supernatural realm as well as in the natural realm.

Over the years we have witnessed how God has miraculously used both supernatural and natural pathways to heal our patients and to demonstrate His marvelous healing and saving power.

I know what God has done in my life, and I know what God has done in the lives of our patients. He can do the same in your life—in fact, He has a unique pathway to healing for you! He is the Lord, who heals you (see Exodus 15:26). By His stripes you were healed (see Isaiah 53:5).

Linda and I are standing with you as you seek God's pathway to healing for a healthy immune system and as you walk in His pathway to total healing for your life.

If you do not know Jesus Christ as your

personal Lord and Savior, I invite you to pray the following prayer and ask Jesus to come into your life:

Lord Jesus, I invite you into my life as my Lord and Savior. I repent of my past sins. I ask you to forgive me. Thank you for shedding your blood on the cross to cleanse me from my sin and to heal me. I receive your gift of everlasting life and surrender all to you. Thank you, Jesus, for saving me. Amen.

ABOUT THE AUTHOR

Reginald B. Cherry, M.D., did his premed at Baylor University, graduated from the University of Texas Medical School, and has practiced diagnostic and preventive medicine for more than twenty-five years. His work in medicine has been recognized and honored by the city of Houston and by President George W. Bush when he was governor of Texas.

Dr. Cherry and his wife, Linda, a clinical nurse who has worked with Dr. Cherry and his patients during the past two-and-a-half decades, now host the popular television program *The Doctor and the Word*, which has a potential weekly viewing audience of 90 million homes. They also publish a monthly medical newsletter and produce topical audiocassette teachings, pocket books, such as this one, and booklets. Dr. Cherry is author of the bestselling books *The Doctor and the Word*, *The Bible Cure*, and *Healing Prayer*.

RESOURCES AVAILABLE FROM REGINALD B. CHERRY MINISTRIES, INC.

Books

Prayers That Heal: Faith-Building Prayers When You Need a Miracle

Combining the wisdom of over twenty-five years of medical practice and the revelation of God's Word, Dr. Cherry provides the knowledge you need to pray effectively against diabetes, cancer, heart disease, eye problems, hypoglycemia, and fifteen other common afflictions that rob you of your health.

Healing Prayer

A fascinating in-depth look at the vital link between spiritual and physical healing. Dr. Cherry presents actual case histories of people healed through prayer, plus the latest information on herbs, vitamins, and supplements that promote vibrant health. This is sound information you need to keep you healthy—mind, soul, and body.

God's Pathway to Healing: Bone Health

Bone mass loss and osteoporosis affect more than 34 million Americans today, and statistics indicate that these numbers will continue to grow dramatically in the decades to come. Though bone disease affects four times the number of women as men, the men who suffer from its complications are often twice as likely to die from them as are women. None of us has room to ignore this debilitating ailment; we all need to do what we can now to either prevent or reverse its effects. In this pocket book, Dr. Cherry shares with readers the things they can do, no matter their age, to strengthen bones and immensely reduce the risk of bone mass loss that results in fractures that can rob us of the quality of life God promised us, if not take life from us altogether. This is a book for all ages and both sexes, as building strong bones is an issue all of us need to address.

God's Pathway to Healing: Diabetes

Diabetes is reaching epidemic proportions as 17 million Americans now face the disease—more than one-third of them not even aware that they have it—and another one million a year will develop it. Some statistics suggest that by the year 2028, one in four Americans will have diabetes. The severe complications of diabetes also give us reason for concern, since it more than triples the risk of death for young adults who acquire it. However, God has a pathway both for prevention and healing of this proliferating disease. In this pocket book, Dr. Cherry outlines the lifestyle changes to prevent and control diabetes as well as the best medications and natural alternatives for reducing its threat to our overall health. This is a book no one can afford to miss, as diabetes most likely affects at least one person you know or love.

God's Pathway to Healing: Digestion

Dr. Cherry discusses keys to a naturally healthy digestive system, including better digestion and absorption of food, proper elimination of waste, and the place of "good" bacteria. He points readers toward better eating habits and natural nutritional supplements to improve digestion.

God's Pathway to Healing: Heart

Heart disease kills twice as many people as all the forms of cancer combined, and more than half of the body of Christ dies of coronary artery or cardiovascular diseases. However, there are things that you can do to keep yourself free of heart disease. An incredible wealth of research in recent years has been done on natural extracts and foods that will feed this muscle and keep it strong and healthy. When these nutrients are combined with faith, prayer, and God's Word, you will find yourself quickly on God's pathway to healing and a healthy heart.

God's Pathway to Healing: Herbs That Heal

Learn the truth about common herbal remedies and discover the possible side effects of each. Discover which herbs can help treat symptoms of insomnia, arthritis, heart problems, asthma, and many other conditions. Read this book and see if herbs are part of God's pathway to healing for you.

God's Pathway to Healing: Joints and Arthritis

Dr. Cherry says painful joints and arthritis do not have to be part of aging. Recent medical breakthroughs show that natural substances can relieve pain and inflammation and slow or prevent cartilage loss.

God's Pathway to Healing: Memory and Mental Acuity

As the baby-boomer generation ages, we are facing more problems with mental function than ever before. Whether it is because of age-related memory loss or poor nutrition or pollutants we take in that affect the way we think and concentrate, people of all ages need new information about how to keep their minds healthy and strong. In this pocket book, Dr. Cherry addresses these concerns in a straightforward and easy-to-understand manner that can help people facing ailments such as depression, attention-deficit hyperactivity disorder (ADHD), migraine headaches, Alzheimer's disease, and many other concerns associated with our brain's function. This book may well be God's key for you to a healthy memory and sharp, focused mind.

God's Pathway to Healing: Menopause

This pocket book is full of helpful advice for women who are going through what potentially can be a very stressful time of life. Find out what foods, supplements, and steps lead to a pathway to healing for menopause and perimenopause.

God's Pathway to Healing: Prostate

This pocket book is packed with enlightening insights for men who are searching for ways to prevent prostate cancer or who have actually been diagnosed with the disease. Discover how foods, plant-derived natural supplements, and a change in diet can be incorporated into your life to help you find a pathway to healing for prostate disease.

God's Pathway to Healing: Vision

Macular degeneration, cataracts, vision degeneration due to complications of diabetes, and other eye conditions can be slowed or prevented. Dr. Cherry discusses herbs and nutritional changes people can make to keep their vision strong.

God's Pathway to Healing: Vitamins and Supplements

With the huge number of supplements and multivitamins on the market today, it is often difficult to know what to take to get what we need and what not to take to make sure we don't get amounts that might be harmful. This easy-to-follow pocket book is a tremendous reference to anyone who wants to stay healthy in this age where new and epidemic diseases seem to be discovered more regularly than ever before. This pocket book could well be the key you need to discovering the miraculous power God has unlocked through natural extracts and nutritional supplements to keep His people healthy and whole to the end of their days on earth.

Dr. Cherry's Little Instruction Book for Health and Healing

This book contains easy-to-read information about healthy habits, natural remedies, and nutritional guidance, along with biblical principles for supernatural healing. Also included are prayers and Scripture as a reminder that God's desire is that His people be healthy. This is a helpful small volume for readers familiar with Dr. Cherry's work and a great introduction for those who are new to his ministry.

The Bible Cure (now in paperback)

Dr. Cherry presents hidden truths in the Bible taken from ancient dietary health laws, how Jesus anointed with natural substances to heal, and how to activate faith through prayer for health and healing. This book validates scientific medical research by using it to reveal God's original health plan.

The Doctor and the Word (now in paperback)

Dr. Cherry introduces the idea of how God has a pathway to healing for everyone. Jesus healed instantaneously as well as through a process. Discover how the manifestation of your healing can come about by seeking His ways.

Dr. Cherry's Study Guides, Volume 2 (bound volume)

Receive thirty valuable resource study guides from topics Dr. Cherry has taught on the Trinity Broadcasting Network (TBN) program *The Doctor and the Word.*

OTHER HELPS

Basic Nutrient Support

Dr. Cherry has developed a daily nutrient supplement that is the simplest to take and yet the most complete supplement available today. Protect your body daily with more than sixty natural substances that fight cancer, heart disease, and many other problems. Call Natural Alternatives at (800) 339-5952 to place your order. Please mention service code "BN30" when ordering. (Or order through the company's Web site: *www.AbundantNutrition.com.*)

Immunity Support

Your immune system is responsible for protecting you from thousands of different types of bacteria, viruses, and other harmful organisms in the environment. But factors such as poor diet, stress, lack of sleep, aging, and nutritional deficiencies can all run your immune system down and make you more susceptible to these germs.

Fortunately, God has given us a plan for optimizing our immunity. As a medical doctor who believes in God's pathway to healing, Dr. Cherry has been able to help many people improve the function of their immune systems by recommending simple changes in diet and lifestyle, and by supplementing their diets with key immune-boosting nutrients.

Now you too can boost your immunity by taking the *Immunity Support* formula. *Immunity Support* is the culmination of twenty-five years of clinical experience and research into nutrition. It contains the twenty-three immune-balancing nutrients, herbs, extracts, and food concentrates that Dr. Cherry recommends for achieving optimal immune function—all in one convenient formula that is safe enough to take every day.

Call Natural Alternatives at (800) 339-5952 to place your order. Please mention service code "BN30" when ordering.

Reginald B. Cherry Ministries, Inc.
P.O. Box 27711
Houston, TX 77227-7711

1-888-DRCHERRY

BECOME A PATHWAY TO HEALING PARTNER

We invite you to become a pathway partner. We ask you to stand with us in prayer and financial support as we provide new programs, resources, books, pocket books, and a unique, one-of-a-kind monthly newsletter.

Our monthly Pathway to Healing Partner newsletter sorts through the confusion about health and healing. In it, Dr. Cherry shares sensible, biblical, and medical steps you can take to get well and stay well. Every issue points you to your pathway to healing. Writing from a Christian physician's Bible-based point of view, Dr. Cherry talks about nutrition and health, how to pray for specific diseases, updates on the latest medical research, Linda's own recipes for healthy eating, and questions and answers about issues you need to know about.

In addition, we'll provide you with Dr. Cherry and Linda's ministry calendar, broadcast schedule, resources for better living, and special monthly offers.

This newsletter is available to you as you partner with the Cherrys through prayer and monthly financial support to help expand this God-given ministry. Pray today about responding with a monthly contribution. Call us or write to the following address to find out how you can receive this valuable information.

Become a pathway partner today by writing
Reginald B. Cherry Ministries, Inc.
P.O. Box 27711
Houston, TX 77227-7711
Or visit our Web site:
www.drcherry.org

1-888-DRCHERRY